KITCHEN INTERIORS

New Spaces and Designs for Cooking and Dining

gestalten

KITCHEN AS CULTURE

Jeppe Christensen

Founder and CEO of the kitchen brand Reform

Kitchens Shaped by Culture

High culture, subculture and counterculture. Designers spend a lot of time thinking about kitchen culture. We at Reform believe that the kitchen acts as a mirror of our current circumstances; it says something about the times in which we live. It reflects changes in culture—in gender roles and family structures, in how we eat and spend time together, how we live in solitude and alongside each other, and what we prefer and prioritize. Kitchen culture is the sum of the people, objects, rituals, and values we human beings bring to the table.

The idea of the kitchen as a mirror is not new, from artist Georgia O'Keeffe's cream-hued kitchenette overlooking the Abiquiú desert to the poetic yet utilitarian nature of architect Lina Bo Bardi's Glass House kitchen. We see it again in the earthy minimalism of Donald Judd's Marfa kitchen with his eccentric tableware collection, or the food writer Richard Olney's deeply rustic Provençal abode, where he hosted legendary dinners for James Baldwin, Julia Child, and other luminaries of his time. The kitchen becomes us. It reflects the culture and tastes of its owner's path, a place and time; it is an intimate portrait.

At Reform, we approach the kitchen as a representation of a meeting between culture and function, as modeled by the Bauhaus movement and its reimagining of the lived environment. We want our work to say something about the human condition; something both universal and particular to the time we live in right now. Our perspective is also that kitchen designs should move toward a more desirable future. Our kitchens always marry functional simplicity with an artistic sensibility, as we believe that great design has the potential to greatly improve people's lives.

But back to culture. The architects and designers we work with—from icons such as Jean Nouvel to contemporary duo Muller Van Severen—create a beautiful and functional framework in which culture unfolds. This mission continues to inform and challenge how we see the kitchen space and all that it can hold—to reframe it.

Double-Sided

Today, we live in a cultural cross-section. A distinct focus on our individuality and, simultaneously, the need to belong to something greater than ourselves. Religious beliefs, political belonging, and nationality all used to play a big part in our identity. These days, we identify and self-express by what we consume, whether that means consuming culture or goods.

The kitchen speaks to this duality. It allows us to express something meaningful about ourselves to the outside world. It is what we want people—family, friends, or even followers—to see. It is a distinctly social context. Simultaneously, it is our most private space, telling a very personal story. The contents of our drawers, our personal routines, our quirks and preferences all reveal something about our inner workings.

A good kitchen design explores this tension between personal and social. From a design perspective, the kitchen has historically been, and is increasingly becoming, a meaningful place to observe how we live, and how that lifestyle evolves.

In Orbit

Kitchen offerings are booming, both high- and low-end. This means we are now likely to choose our own kitchen with unparalleled autonomy. The increasingly democratic nature of design allows us to venture beyond the standardized. To make choices with intention. For many, the kitchen has become a personal sort of jewelry to the home, the ultimate document of who we really are and what we stand for.

Historically, the kitchen was a mere tool. Situated on the periphery of a home, it used to be a purely functional place for the preparation of food. A stop on the way to the final destination—the living or dining room. Nowadays, the architect starts by placing the kitchen and plans the rest from there. It is the centerpiece that sets the order of a home. A core, a heart.

We are a part of the repeating path. The kitchen is there first thing in the morning, throughout the workday, when we invite people over and when we turn off the lights at night. No room

encompasses life so fully, with such versatility. It has never been more central, neither has it held as many functions as it does today. Its purpose is no longer just cooking; it is creating a compelling atmosphere for being with people.

A Teacher

Remarkably, the kitchen plays two parts: it is both a room and furniture. It is something we constantly interact with and experience through our senses and body. For many of us, it is the design object or space that teaches us the most about the importance of good design, functionality, and aesthetics, and how these intersect.

It makes sense that it is the design object we invest the most in, both economically and personally. Many will tell you that getting it right is emotionally demanding, but immensely rewarding. Few of us ever get a chance to participate in the making of a design, to make choices based on both intuition and intimate knowledge of our own being. Building or even choosing a kitchen might be the closest we all get to becoming architects or designers. It means participating in its making.

The Pull of the Kitchen

The kitchen has rightfully become a priority. These days, it is not only where we cook, entertain, and connect with each other. It is also where we work, craft, read, and so much more. It has taken on a whole new meaning, becoming a sort of workshop; our tools are all gathered here—for cooking, socializing, working and unwinding.

This recent reordering of the home means that the center of gravity has shifted. While the TV was the central design piece of a late 20th-century home, you could argue that the kitchen has toppled it. Ironically, screens are still very much present in our lives. Perhaps that is why we are now gravitating toward communal spaces that awake the senses, that bring us back into our bodies. The kitchen offers a meaningful framework for that.

People are losing so many natural spaces for physical interaction, which is why many of us now

want to reconnect with the senses and particularly the sense of touch. While architects and designers have long argued for the crucial role of tactility in our lived environment, we are now certain of its impact on our greater sense of well-being.

Good design speaks to the senses. Though they might seem like small gestures—the particular feel of wood or the right handle of a cabinet, the way the choice of light or color underscores a particular mood—these conscious design decisions make the kitchen a profound arena to experiment with and experience the effect design has on our minds and bodies. It allows us to experience a space and design an object with our entire being, through our sense of taste, smell, sound, touch, and sight. A kitchen marries the senses in a logical and poetic way. Perhaps that is why people hover around the kitchen at a party, or linger after breakfast, reluctant to start the day. It is a refuge from an overwhelming exterior world, a familiar comfort in the face of uncertainty. It is where we are closest to ourselves and one another.

Everyday Potential

Today, everything is self-presentation, the kitchen included. How we shape and put our mark on this space is the most intricate way of telling the story of ourselves. A chair is a chapter, while the kitchen is a full blown universe, the whole book. It is exceptional but, most importantly, it is also everyday. It is commonplace, everyone has one. That is what makes it so approachable and human, something we can all read or write ourselves into.

A kitchen is always in transformation, much like us. We transform it with our whole being—the things we touch or lean into, the way we move in it, the way we use it. Surfaces age gracefully, or less so, with time. Objects move in, or out. Some seem to always have been there, even before us. People come and go, pass through. Memories are amassed and feel chiseled into the very fabric of it.

The kitchen holds the potential of time. It supports and comforts us as we ourselves transform, similarly refined over time.

A TESTING GROUND FOR A STUDIO'S ECLECTIC STYLE

Highbury Apartment · Holloway Li · London, United Kingdom

Inspired by the local London vernacular of fast-food joints, the "kebab-shop kitchen" is a sleek stainless-steel design that lines one wall of an open-plan living space (which also features a bathtub). The design studio Holloway Li has used this apartment as a testing ground for its ideas. The scheme establishes a comfortable transition from old to new; though resolutely contemporary, the apartment retains several original Victorian features, such as the butterfly roof in the living room and plaster moldings in the entryway. At the same time, the convergence of high and low culture is in evidence. The color palette is brash, with moldings painted in a rich blue, and though the kitchen evokes memories of a good night out on the town, its curved backsplash lends the design an elegance that finds echoes in the sculptural limestone skirting that lines the room. Holloway Li's furnishings populate the apartment, including a striking resin dining table and its bulbous T4 chair.

NOGUCHI

From the raw, exposed plaster and warm Douglas fir to the stark stainless steel and crisp micro-cement, surfaces are tactile and with a varied palette, serving as the perfect backdrop for the citrus-colored furnishings.

CLEVER STORAGE TO MAKE USE OF EVERY SPACE

Maison pour Dodo · Studio Merlin · London, United Kingdom

This renovated apartment, in a style that Studio Merlin calls "warm minimalism," combines clever storage solutions with Scandinavian design resulting in a light, airy, and clutter-free environment. What had been two separate rooms on the second floor is now a large L-shaped space with light flooding from the front and rear of the house. A Douglas fir floor provides a sense of continuity as you move from the living room to the kitchen. To make good use of even the most unpromising spaces, Studio Merlin has introduced wall-to-wall, floor-to-ceiling shelving and cabinetry throughout. In the kitchen, utilities—including the sink—are integrated within cabinets with dark-blue fronts. Shelving lines the alcoves and there is an informal recessed sitting space at one end of the countertop. All the lines are flush and minimal. Colors are warm and calm and many of the furnishings have smooth rounded edges, which fulfills the client's brief to "create a soft-feeling apartment that minimizes material anxiety and visual noise."

INDIA
Nigel Slater

The design of the apartment borrows from Scandinavian style, seen in the clean lines of the open shelving and, in particular, the application of one strong color juxtaposed with the softer, warmer tones of whitewashed wood.

A SERIES OF DISTINCT SPACES

Mo-tel House · Office S&M · London, United Kingdom

You don't often find a canary-yellow I-beam spanning the ceiling in a kitchen, but that is what you will see at Mo-tel House, a remodeling of a previously damp, dark, and cramped lower ground floor in a Victorian London townhouse. The clients gave Office S&M a simple brief: to create a space full of surprises and delight for each member of their young family to enjoy. With plinths to climb, soft surfaces for nestling, and tiny spaces to crawl into, S&M's scheme for this open-plan, dual-aspect kitchen and dining space does not disappoint. At its heart, a pink and blue bench with a crested canopy provides seating and storage and doubles as a cozy reading nook—essentially something for each member of the family. Designed by the architects and rendered in cotton-candy colors, all the furniture here has an architectural aesthetic, as if constructed from a huge set of children's building blocks. Throughout the design, a clever use of mirrors and lighting reflects and frames views, distorting scale and suggesting worlds beyond.

Much of the furniture is built-in, with each unit designed to be a small piece of architecture in its own right. Shape and color help to define each area of the room, creating a series of interconnected but distinct spaces.

A WUNDERKAMMER IN THE HEART OF THE CITY

Font 6 Apartment · Serboli Bureau, Colombo Architecture, and Margherita Serboli Arquitectura · Barcelona, Spain

This compact apartment lies a stone's throw from Barcelona's Sagrada Familia. Although housed in an art nouveau building, the original space was poorly configured and in a state of disrepair; many of its original features were unsalvageable. In renovating the place, the architects took the bold decision to rip out existing walls and create an entirely new living space. At its core, and framed by an arched passageway, a box lined with blue lacquered tongue-and-groove wood houses a bathroom, while also serving to define the spaces around it. It is one wall of this box that forms the back wall of the kitchen in the open-plan living space, with the blue wood echoed in the kitchen island and undercounter cabinets (the styling repeats once more in the bedroom). The kitchen styling is minimal. Appliances are fully integrated to hide them from view. Flush, handleless cabinets are topped with Portobello marble countertops and backsplash, each shaped with gentle curves to match those that frame the blue box.

AIMING HIGH WITH A HALL OF MIRRORS

Lardo Lyma · Dries Otten · Antwerp, Belgium

This kitchen occupies a room toward the rear of a 19th-century residence in Antwerp, and lies adjacent to a winter garden, a dining room, and the hallway. By housing major facilities—oven, stovetop, and sink—in a semi-island at the center of the room, Dries Otten architects have maintained plenty of circulation in the room but have also maximized on the amount of storage space available. The design features almost wall-to-wall cabinetry and a bench with extra storage, as well as a working space overlooking the garden. The room has relatively low ceilings, so to add height, Dries Otten settled on a simple but effective interior design that divides the walls horizontally into three bands. The first is low-level terra-cotta-colored wainscotting that ties the different zones of the kitchen together. Above this are plain white cupboard doors, which contrast nicely with the richly veined marble countertops. And finally, on top, is a strip of mirrored panels reminiscent of a fairground hall of mirrors.

STAY
SORTED
WITH
PROPER
STORAGE
PLANNING

In less formal kitchens, the layout often includes rails with hooks, wall-mounted plate racks, and open shelves for storing everyday cooking equipment and utensils.
Below: Studio Hoka in Warsaw makes clever use of storage space beneath a flight of stairs.

No matter what size a kitchen, or how often it is used, it needs storage space. The key lies in assessing how much you need, what form it will take, and how to balance it within the overall layout.

The kitchen is a working space that needs to be well organized and clutter-free. That means dedicating adequate space to the storage of pots, pans, and utensils, cooking ingredients, plates, glasses, cutlery, and more—there is no end to the paraphernalia a person might have, depending on how serious they are about cooking, and how many mouths there are to feed. Calculating the right amount of storage space depends on the number of people in a household and how regularly cooking takes place. With that established, there are many clever options for making the best use of the available space, ranging from wall-to-wall cabinetry through free-standing dressers and cupboards to open shelves, trolleys, racks, and drawers. Most kitchens involve a combination that keeps everyday items at arm's length and less frequently used items in harder-to-reach spaces. Crucially, it is the styling of the storage that most influences the overall look of the room—paneled oak cupboards for a country kitchen, a stainless-steel rack for an industrial look, and doors with brightly colored laminates for a more youthful vibe.

Whether wall-mounted or freestanding, open shelves make for easy access and are one of the most economical ways of storing multiple ingredients or stacking crockery while taking up relatively little space.

Drawers—especially those with dividers—offer the best way to keep small utensils and cutlery neatly organized. Some prefer to include a built-in or walk-in pantry that keeps everyday ingredients close at hand but concealed from view.

STORAGE SOLUTIONS IN A MULTIUSE SPACE

Studio H · Studio Hoka · Warsaw, Poland

This clever renovation of an atelier in Warsaw is all about smart storage solutions. Making maximum use of a 14 ft (4.3 m) ceiling, Karolina Howorko of Studio Hoka extended upward to add a mezzanine level for sleeping and working. In doing so she has increased the space in the apartment by almost a third, allowing for a more generous living space below. Largely inspired by Japanese design, as well as train and boat interiors, Howorko has optimized every square foot of the apartment, introducing built-in storage that allows the living space to function variously as a kitchen, dining room, living room—or any combination of the three—simply by drawing a curtain, pulling out a tabletop, or stowing a couple of stools. The kitchen is at the center of the apartment but does not dominate it. Outward appearances suggest it is a modest, three-unit affair with sink, oven, and a couple of cupboards. In fact, it also houses a dishwasher and a fridge, the latter concealed behind a door in the stairs.

A HUMBLE KITCHEN FOR MINIMAL USE

MCS Apartment · Serboli Bureau and Colombo Architecture · Barcelona, Spain

For the renovation of this Barcelona apartment, Serboli Bureau's and Colombo Architecture's remit had three elements: to redefine the main living space to make better sense of the layout; to install an unobtrusive kitchen for minimal use; and to maximize the natural light entering the building. The architects' solution to all three lay in the installation of three self-contained units. The first of these is, essentially, a bank of floor-to-ceiling kitchen cabinets with a cutaway section lined in heavily figured marble. Facing it, and similarly cut-away and lined with marble, the second unit is simply equipped with a sink, stovetop, and oven. Both are clad in brushed aluminum and are highly sophisticated, almost sculptural, in appearance. The third unit spans the rear wall of the living space, separating it from the apartment's more private rooms. Finished in a sleek blue-black lacquer, the unit serves as a dramatic back-drop to the bright new kitchen, while a central mirrored section reflects light back from the large living room windows at the opposite end of the room.

RAW AND NATURAL MATERIALS

Apartment R405 · Zly architekt · Bratislava, Slovakia

This relatively compact studio space near the center of Bratislava was designed by Zly architekt as part of a wider initiative to revitalize abandoned inner-city industrial areas. According to the architects, their design is "about a feeling of openness and simplicity, about atmospheres and views." A transparent partition separates the kitchen/living room from the bedroom, allowing you to perceive and enjoy the whole depth of the space all at once. Inspired by modern Japanese design, the kitchen is resolutely modular and minimalist, with an emphasis on raw and natural materials. The lower row of cabinets is made from plywood and sits beneath a shorter run of mirror-fronted cupboards. Between them, the wall is lined with a basic glazed white tile. At the far end of the kitchen, a set of shelves rendered in a striking green makes for a bold statement. The focus on raw and natural materials runs throughout the apartment with the plywood cabinetry repeated in the bedroom and the tiling continued in the bathroom, giving the styling of the apartment a clear continuity throughout.

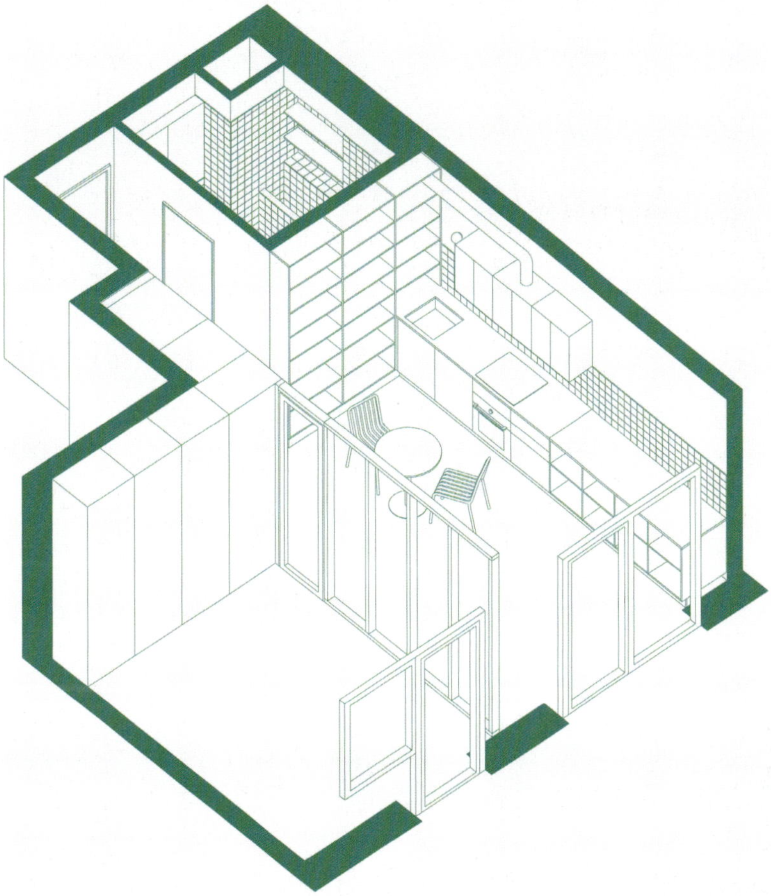

Materiality is key to the success of this utilitarian, almost industrial, design. It is borne out in the limited color palette, the use of industrial materials such as glass, mirror, and tiles, and the lack of surface decoration on modular units

SIMPLE, SUSTAINABLE PERFECTION WITH PLYWOOD

Curve Appeal · nimtim architects · London, United Kingdom

In response to a brief to increase natural light levels and improve the connectivity and coherence of this 1920s semi-detached house, nimtim architects settled on a novel solution based on a single joinery element. Installed wall to wall, fashioned from plywood, and featuring a repeating curved motif, the joinery frees up the spaces around it by providing alcoves, shelves, and cupboards to house objets d'art, books, and crockery. Truly multifunctional, it also serves as a room partition with large sliding doors; as a fire separation to the upstairs rooms; and as a family crafting area. Here and there, playful cutout windows allow glimpses into adjacent spaces. In the kitchen, the plywood is complemented by handmade terra-cotta floor tiles, white Formica countertops, and a tiled backsplash to create a space that is simultaneously warm and tactile and clean, bright, and highly functional. All materials are also low cost and sustainable, demonstrating that high-quality architectural interventions can be made with relatively little financial or environmental impact.

PART-TIME
OTTOLENGHI SIMPLE
PLENTY
THE MODERN LARDER
JERUSALEM
PLENTY MORE
TOM KERRIDGE
SWEET

OTTOLENGHI SIMPLE
PLENTY
THE MODERN LARDER

There is an emphasis on sustainability in the use of materials here. The plywood is low VOC and formaldehyde-free, and the handmade terra-cotta tiles were fired using by-products such as almond shells and olive pits instead of fossil fuels.

A SENSE OF CONTINUITY AT EVERY LEVEL

Bespoke Kitchen and Study · Uncommon Projects · London, United Kingdom

During a major renovation and extension of this Victorian house in London, Uncommon Projects created a bespoke kitchen, styled to connect the house on three levels. The playful design centers on a wall of birch plywood cabinetry with American white oak veneer that starts at basement level and extends through the double-height kitchen to a study on the mezzanine floor above. At basement level, cupboard doors are lacquered in dark gray, creating a monolithic feel that grounds the scheme both visually and spatially. Above the countertop, the wall unit becomes a series of shelves with brightly colored sliding doors. As it rises, the unit creates a common visual thread through the house and a sense of continuity from one floor to the next. At the heart of the kitchen, standing on a black tiled floor, an island marks the social point of the space. A series of deep and shallow drawers, open shelves, and sliding doors provide versatile storage space and create a different look on all four sides.

Moving away from the ubiquitous minimalist white kitchen, the greatest challenge the architects faced was to create a design language that unified the whole space while giving each of the three areas its own identity and function.

A SPACE WITH INDUSTRIAL UNDERTONES

Victorian Terrace Family Kitchen · Pluck · London, United Kingdom

Set within a bright, spacious room toward the rear of a Victorian row house in London, this bespoke kitchen combines a wall of Pluck cabinetry with a stainless-steel countertop and a glazed tile backsplash. Paired with a chunky wooden dining table, mismatched chairs, and a long, plush sofa up against the far wall, the effect is to create a cozy, informal space with clean, almost industrial undertones. The flush-fronted cabinets with recessed handles have a geometric configuration and a matte finish that contributes to the industrial look, as does the integrated sink, which gives a smooth transition with the countertop and no joins. These elements are balanced by a wooden cabinet with fluted glass doors and Pluck's Spoke open shelving—a design inspired by Victorian bamboo furniture. Combined with the soft shades of pink and green used for the glazed tiling and matte cabinetry, these elements introduce a softer, more rustic feel to the kitchen, achieving an overall sense of harmony.

Built-in cabinetry including a much-coveted Pluck pantry occupies two of the room's walls. The owners favored a table rather than an island, allowing them more flexibility in the room's layout.

A HARMONIOUS BLEND OF STAINLESS STEEL AND WOOD

Magpie House · DGN Studio · London, United Kingdom

This kitchen, installed as part of a renovation and extension of a Victorian row house in Hackney, east London, is a carefully crafted piece of furniture that brings together both the old and the new. DGN Studio's brief was to create a hard-working, practical kitchen with an open plan that has everything on show instead of hidden away. Inspired by the catering kitchens of local Turkish restaurants, the design combines a wall of stainless steel with a wooden framework and door fronts made of solid ash sourced from a forest in Lithuania. The sink is welded into the work surface, which is also stainless steel. The styling runs through into the dining room, creating more shelves for glassware and crockery. The design is set against walls of exposed, white-washed brick and a polished concrete floor. With a skylight directly above, the warm, textured tones of the woodwork balance with the coolness of the stainless steel to evoke a unified industrial feel in this bright, airy, open-plan space.

As many reclaimed materials as possible were used to create a space that feels neither new or old, and that shares a design language with the existing building and the garden studio beyond.

THE BEATING HEART OF AN ECOSYSTEM

Gutshof Güldenhof · Heim Balp Architekten · Stechlin, Germany

This kitchen lies at the center of an arts complex conceived by an internationally renowned conceptual artist and realized by Berlin-based Heim Balp Architekten. The land was originally part of a farm, and Heim Balp worked with the existing buildings to create an art studio, exhibition spaces, and workshops, as well as apartments, a conservatory, and communal spaces—essentially all the facilities required for developing a sustainable, self-sufficient ecosystem. Several of the original stone stables and barns have been repurposed, as has the old farmworkers' residence, which now houses the kitchen. Painted black in contrast to the stone buildings, the structure has a new roof made of corrugated metal, in a nod to typical 20th-century rural structures. The kitchen acts as a hub for social interaction for the people who live there and their guests, underpinning the spirit of the entire complex. Spacious yet highly functional, it serves the community day in and day out. Minimal, utilitarian, and solid, it is very much a tool rather than a piece of design.

In repurposing the existing structures of the old farming complex, the architects were able to develop the full potential of the site, ensuring the activities of the community remained fully embedded within the natural surroundings.

A NEW TAKE ON ARTS AND CRAFTS STYLING

Arts and Crafts Home · Spaces by Hollie Velten · Maplewood, NJ, USA

Richly grained wood accents, beautifully patterned wall coverings, and artisan tiles are the hallmarks of this restyled kitchen in an American Arts and Crafts home. The clients were installing a new deVol kitchen and enlisted the services of Spaces by Hollie Velten to ensure that the interior design maintained the aesthetics of the home's original styling. In an L-shaped unit flanking two walls of the kitchen, simple, bone-colored cabinet and drawer fronts with brass pulls sit beneath a marble countertop with an inset butler's sink at the center of one run and a gas range in the other. Above the stove is a tiled backsplash and a brass rail hung with copper cookware. In the adjoining spaces, the palette sets earthy, natural greens, yellows, and pinks against the dark wood of the paneled walls, which also feature checkered tiled sections and floral wallpaper. Emphasizing "human qualities and imperfections with character," the designer handpicked materials like artisan tiles and hand-drawn wallpaper designs, eschewing anything overly trendy.

This classic kitchen design pairs traditional paneled cabinets with more modern touches, such as the brass fittings and open shelving. The new elements sit alongside copperware, earthenware, and wooden utensils to reinforce the Arts and Crafts aesthetic.

COHESION THROUGH COLORS AND PATTERNS

Epping Forest Cottage Kitchen · Pluck · Essex, United Kingdom

The success of this kitchen design by London-based Pluck studio lies in combining new pared-back cabinetry and furniture with existing elements to create a space that looks both contemporary and traditional at the same time. At one end of the room, a window set within a wall of striking floral wallpaper is flanked with runs of low-level cabinetry that incorporate a butler's sink, a range, and a free-standing refrigerator. Each run has a recycled-glass terrazzo countertop and tiled backsplash, above which much-needed storage space is provided by a set of Pluck's Spoke shelves on one side and a large plate rack on the other—solutions that prevent this relatively narrow end of the room from feeling too hemmed in. At the opposite end of the room, wall-to-wall cabinetry incorporates a built-in pantry. A clever color palette unites the various elements, with a bold blue-and-white checkered floor picking out the stronger tones in the floral wallpaper while the more subtle tones find echoes in the soft Ruskin Blossom color chosen for the cabinetry.

The designers carefully maintained a "cottage" aesthetic in this kitchen—from the simple spun-aluminum pendant lights and chunky wooden table with a set of Windsor chairs to the brass rail with hooks for hanging mismatched cups.

Epping Forest Cottage Kitchen

AN INVITING FEELING— RUSTIC AND WHIMSICAL

Deerhyrst Kitchen · Molly Mahon · Forest Row, United Kingdom

Deerhyrst Cottage is the home of British printmaker Molly Mahon, so it should come as no surprise to find it full of beautiful, block-printed fabrics in a harmonious range of cheerful, welcoming colors. For Mahon, the kitchen is the true heart of the home. It is where she and her family spend much of their time, and it is important to her that it is comfortable as well as practical. The room has a mix of design styles, largely driven by budget. At its heart stands an Everhot stove and, across the room, a pretty old dresser stacked with a collection of colorful and patterned tableware. "It's like having a piece of art on a wall," says Mahon. Beneath a countertop made of scaffolding planks, hand-block-printed curtains with pretty scalloping open to reveal rustic, blue-painted shelves. The curtains, along with the window blinds and soft furnishings in an adjacent sitting area, were all made by Mahon. For her, adding layers of color, pattern, and texture in this way helps to achieve the cozy, warm, and inviting atmosphere that she loves.

In a space that is constantly evolving, Molly Mahon draws on inspiration from Georgian farmhouses, Shaker-style kitchens, and the nearby property Charleston, the former home and studio of Bloomsbury Group designers Vanessa Bell and Duncan Grant.

Things need to pack
BEN FOGLE

CREATIVE APPROACH TO KITCHENS ON A BUDGET

Above (left): In this compact apartment in Barcelona, precious materials such as marble and brass are mixed with more basic elements to generate a feeling of affordable luxury. Below: For their FlagFlat in Spain, architects Rosana Galián and Alejandro Martínez collaborated with a local carpenter specializing in cabinetmaking.

Designing a kitchen on a tight budget does not mean that you cannot have the kitchen of your dreams—it just means that you have to prioritize your needs and consider your options more carefully from the outset.

The budget kitchen can take several forms. Building from scratch brings the advantages of deciding what's most important—high-end branded appliances, stylish decorative finishes, a fully integrated look, for example—and using that as a starting point. It may be that savings can be made in the amount of space allocated to the kitchen, in buying non-branded appliances, and in seeking out clever storage solutions.

If working within an existing space, obvious ways to save on spending are to minimize any structural work and avoid the relocation of essential services such as water, gas, electricity, and waste disposal. The most resourceful designers relish the opportunity to source low-cost options for cabinetry, furnishings, and lighting, and these are often the things that give a design personality. Quite often, a budget design makes good use of sustainable, locally sourced materials, or finds ways to revive existing elements and recycle materials to give the kitchen a fresh look. There are hundreds of options out there; it is often just a case of applying a little lateral thinking.

Costs can be kept low by adding new fronts to existing or budget carcasses.
In some cases, this allows money to be spent on one stand-out piece (above right).
All sorts of savings can be made by introducing clever storage solutions (below).

The most basic, affordable materials can be used in innovative ways. Simple wooden planks for open shelving (above); pegboard as a backsplash (below left); and standard glazed tiles paired with plywood (below right) all contribute to a unique design.

A NEAT, SIMPLE DESIGN WITH A SCANDINAVIAN AESTHETIC

Allotment Kitchen · Reform · Amager Strand, Denmark

When the owners of a Danish allotment house were looking to upgrade an 11-year-old Ikea kitchen, Reform's modular Basis system proved to be the perfect choice. Inspired by the architect-designed kitchens of midcentury Scandinavia, units are simple, flush-fronted, and available in a range of sizes to allow for a multitude of configurations. The kitchen accounts for almost half the floor plan of the dwelling, and the owners use it regularly throughout the warmer months for outdoor entertaining. Given the humble nature of the building, the kitchen does not need to be highly functional, but with its pastel palette, it does have great style. Set against a pale-green wall, the units have a linoleum finish in a soft pink (called Powder), and the countertop, also finished in linoleum, is Midnight Blue to match the painted exterior of the house. A particularly cute feature of the design are the round handles on the doors and drawers, where each has been carpenter-milled to reveal a tiny disk of wood grain.

Linoleum was the perfect finish for this kitchen, as it is a highly durable organic material that matches the allotment setting. The whitewashed tongue-and-groove walls and wooden floorboards help to keep the space light and bright.

A GALLEY-STYLE KITCHEN WITH A NORDIC EDGE

Frame Kitchen · Reform · Copenhagen, Denmark

When the time came for Christina Zemanova to replace a 1970s kitchen in her Copenhagen home, she sought inspiration from Reform, a studio that specializes in architect-designed kitchens at the modular level. For Zemanova, the answer lay in the Frame kitchen, designed by Stockholm-based studio Note. Distinctly Scandinavian, the cabinetry is understated and geometric and features oak-veneered panels set within a frame with a characteristic triangular profile—hence the system's name. Pairing cupboards with open shelves, the resulting design was perfect for Zemanova's needs and really opened up what was a relatively small, north-facing space. Her desire was to use natural materials in a surprising color, and she opted for a light-blue finish on the cabinets, which she says reminds her of the crisp Danish sky that she can see from the kitchen in winter. Appliances are integrated to keep the appearance of the kitchen clean-lined and calm, and a white marble countertop with light-gray figuring completes the look.

Zemanova kept an eye on practicalities while working with Reform, opting for open shelves beneath the window so that her children can reach crockery for themselves. The painted cabinetry can be refreshed in years to come, creating a new look at little expense.

FEAST
MAMA AFRIKA
POLPO
COOK BEAUTIFUL
OSTERIA 16

TAKING INSPIRATION FROM PROFESSIONAL CATERING SPACES

Loft · Kilo/Honč · Bratislava, Slovakia

This scheme, designed by Bratislava-based architects Kilo/Honč, is the ultimate bachelor pad. One large space is divided into areas for eating, sleeping, bathing, and relaxing—all open to each other and interlinked. The bedroom, for example, is in the middle, screened off with glass partitions and shelved walls. On one side it is open to the kitchen; to the rear it leads to the bathroom. Almost all surfaces in the apartment are finished in raw concrete, while a wall of windows and a bank of shelves raised on slender legs lie behind light, gauzy curtains, bringing a sense of ethereal lightness to the space. In keeping with the theme, the kitchen, which occupies the back wall of the apartment, is inspired by professional catering spaces, with a focus on being unfussy and low maintenance. The material of choice is stainless steel—durable, clean, and functional—and there is no attempt to conceal appliances since the kitchen's functionality is paramount and integral to the design. There are no overhead cabinets. Instead, all kitchen utensils are stacked for easy access on a big open rack, just as they might be in a restaurant kitchen.

Kilo/Honč have succeeded in creating an incredibly versatile apartment, given its relatively small footprint. While some rooms such as the kitchen and bathroom are fixed, the owner has great freedom in how to utilize the remaining spaces.

A SCULPTURAL KITCHEN FOR A QUIRKY RENOVATION

BSP20 House · Raúl Sánchez Architects · Barcelona, Spain

This inspired renovation of a narrow, four-story 19th-century house in Barcelona is the work of architect Raúl Sánchez. When he found it, the building was in a poor state of repair, with little worth salvaging. After completely gutting the place, retaining only the facades, structural walls, and roof slab, Sánchez began to reconstruct the interior. Leaving the rough masonry walls exposed, Sánchez introduced new floor slabs that reach just short of the main facades. Toward the front facade Sánchez inserted a sheet of glass so that you can see all the way down the house from the top; at the rear the space is occupied by a new spiral staircase. The kitchen is on the ground floor, immediately upon entering the house. Set on a mosaic floor—a Barcelona staple—the kitchen is formed of a single unit with integrated appliances. The cupboard fronts are finished with brushed brass and the countertop is marble, giving the whole thing a sculptural feel against the bare-brick walls.

SET THE MOOD WITH GREAT KITCHEN LIGHTING

Simple round globes of white glass mounted or suspended from brass fittings work perfectly with the styling of this London apartment, described by architect Studio Merlin as "warm minimalism." Below: In contrast, the brash and brassy custom-made piece in Studio Alexander Fehre's high-end kitchen exudes "Italian material elegance."

When it comes to lighting, the kitchen is one of the most demanding rooms in the house. More than any other room, it is used multiple times throughout the day for activities that need both direct and diffuse light.

Light in a kitchen can be a complex business, since many kitchens combine food preparation with dining. In a room that benefits from plenty of natural daylight, both activities are straightforward. Come nighttime and the preparation of an evening meal, however, alternatives need to be in place. Yet the kinds of light needed for food preparation—bright and directional—are not always conducive to sitting down and eating a meal in a relaxed, informal environment. The solution lies in devising a system that incorporates both task and ambient lighting in the most appropriate places. For making meals—and washing up after them—bright, directional lighting will avoid the risk of injury and not-quite-scrubbed-enough plates. Because it tends to be less attractive, such lighting is often concealed within the framework of the kitchen cabinetry. For dining, a more subtle, ambient light is achieved through low-hung pendants with decorative shades that create a more diffuse light. Having the option to dim lights can also significantly alter the mood.

Lights suspended over a dining table are most successful when they give off a diffuse light and have a more decorative design that fits in with the overall decor of the space. Lights suspended over a work surface are often more industrial in design, with wide metal fixtures for a brighter glow.

Kitchens can benefit from natural daylight in many ways. Often located in ground floor extensions, they might have skylights in the roof, patio doors that open onto a garden, or floor-to ceiling windows that allow light to flood in.

OPLOS
KOFFIE

A ROOM THAT IS ALL ABOUT THE VIEW

House hkZ · Blaf architecten · Zoersel, Belgium

In this private house development by Blaf architecten, the primary living spaces—the kitchen, dining room, and living room—are arranged in a large, open-plan, split-level volume. Light floods in from windows on all sides, and the numerous views across the house differ according to where you are standing. The kitchen occupies one end of the lower level and is open to the dining area, which itself leads to an outdoor terrace. The living area is perpendicular to the dining room/kitchen on the half-floor above. Exposed timber beams span the ceiling throughout, reinforcing the continuity as you circulate the space. There is a great sense of transparency and fluidity. The kitchen itself comprises a run of low, chestnut-brown cabinets flanking the external wall, which then turns the corner and culminates in a protruding triangular countertop with an inset stovetop. The space is interrupted by a door to a terrace, then continues into the dining room, where cabinets line the wall. The appliances—oven, fridge, dishwasher—are not visible, but surface-mounted extraction pipes and large, bare-bulb pendant lights give the space a semi-industrial feel.

KOFFIE

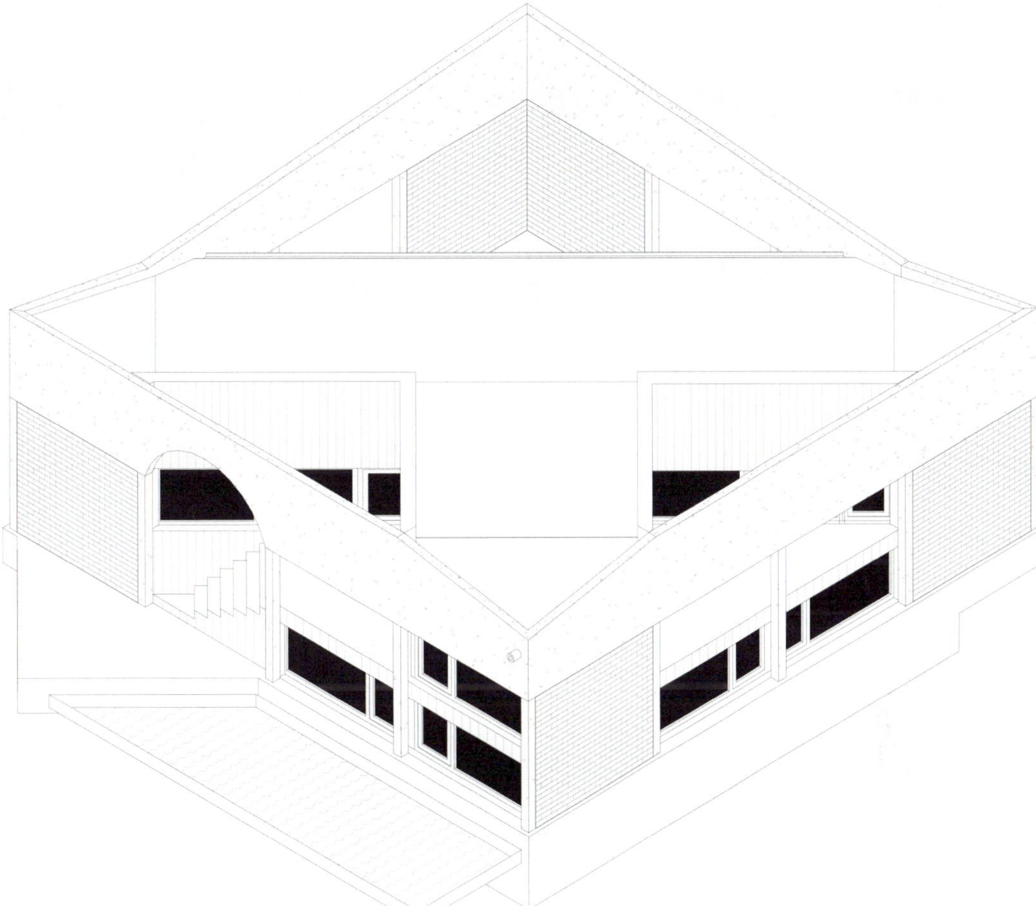

The drawing of the house reveals its complex structure and shows how the internal and external spaces are intertwined. Different sightlines and perspectives unfold within the home to ensure maximum contact with the environment.

ITALIAN ELEGANCE AND PRECISION CUSTOM-BUILDING

House on Achalm · Studio Alexander Fehre · Baden Wuerttemberg, Germany

This stylish, sumptuous design is the work of Stuttgart-based Studio Alexander Fehre. Commissioned to style a sizable, high-end living, kitchen, and dining space for a large family, the studio's brief had two elements. On the one hand, it needed to accommodate a highly functional kitchen and a spacious dining area. On the other, it needed to satisfy the client's wish to reflect a more international approach to interior design. The studio took as its starting point what it calls an "Italian kind of material elegance," and blended it with the sort of precision custom-building found in luxury yachts. Key to the design is the walnut paneling that starts in the dining room and carries through to the kitchen. Primarily decorative in the dining room, with niches created for displaying objects, the wood paneling is used for the fronts of cupboards and drawers in the kitchen and is seamlessly integrated with the cooking appliances. With its vertical slats and rounded edges, it wraps the walls in warmth and creates a sense of flow from one space to the next.

The light fixtures add grace and elegance to the design. In the dining room, smoked glass pendants hang above a marble-topped table, while the kitchen island sits beneath an impressive custom-made fixture with a brass-like finish.

HARMONY IN THE CZECH MOUNTAINS

Glass Cabin · Mjölk architekti · Polubný, Czech Republic

This reconstruction of a 130-year-old cottage blends the old with the new and places the kitchen center stage. To the original building, constructed from locally sourced granite and wood, Mjölk architekti have added glass, using it to build a first-floor extension that spans the rear elevation of the house at ground level. At the boundary between the old and the new—a division emphasized by a change in level—stands the kitchen. Freestanding counters cluster around a large tiled unit with built-in stoves that unites the living room, kitchen, and dining room. From the kitchen, views span the living room and dining room, but also the meadowed landscape outside. The choice of materials aims to strike a balance between tradition and modernity, while maintaining a sense of harmony but also contrast. Harmony, for example, lies in the oak veneer of the kitchen cabinets, which ties them to the timber elements of the original cottage. Contrast, however, can be found in the brass-lined ceiling in the living room, which has the most dramatic effect on mood as the light changes through the day.

By adding a glass "box" to the rear of the house, Mjölk architekti have flooded the living room and kitchen with light while opening vistas across the meadow landscape beyond. At times, the boundary between outside and inside disappears.

BIG CITY VIBES IN A SMALL KITCHEN

Mexico City Residence · Ayromloo Design · Mexico City, Mexico

When asked about her approach to sourcing kitchen appliances for this Mexican apartment, LA-based designer Jessica Ayromloo replies that they were "the most petite and minimal possible." This neat little kitchenette needed to house no more than a little fridge, a sink, and a stovetop for very occasional use. It occupies a space in a large open-plan room that also serves as a dining and living area and is characterized by a vibrant, colorful styling that Ayromloo describes as "industrial vintage modern." Located right in the heart of Mexico City's Centro Histórico, this apartment's interior design takes inspiration from the locale and blends ornate ironwork with terra-cotta stone walls and blockwork tiling. The kitchen itself is made from stainless steel, softened by cabinets with cork fronts. Cork also features as one of the flooring materials. The countertop extends beyond the wall and into the room, and in order to make this feel less obtrusive, Ayromloo gave it a rounded end and a fabric "skirt" in a yellow that matches the surrounding tiles.

AN APPLICATION OF PIGMENTED CONCRETE

The House Recast · Studio Ben Allen · London, United Kingdom

The standout feature of this extension to a Victorian row house in London is Studio Ben Allen's innovative use of pigmented and patterned concrete. Cast offsite and used both structurally and decoratively inside and out, the material allowed the architects to create an original design in which strong shapes and a range of bold, earthy colors come to the fore. In the kitchen, the concrete is molded into a short flight of stairs, a sculptural island, and a long countertop with an integrated sink, both in a rich burnt-orange color. Above, structural elements are rendered in an earthy green and a curved staircase in a striking blue. The same orange and green feature in the extension's rear elevation, and the green structural elements with a scalloped pattern are echoed in a grill set into the orange concrete facade. Back inside, a skylight above the kitchen floods the room with light and has vaulted louvers that create constantly shifting light and shade in the room as the sun moves across the sky.

At the kitchen end of the vaulted, louvered skylight—above the kitchen island—the ceiling opens up to become a double-height space with a mezzanine that connects to the main staircase. It is a feature that allows light to enter deep into the house.

ECCENTRIC PLAY WITH COLOR AND PERSPECTIVE

Venetian Penthouse · Federico Masotto Architecte · Venice, Italy

This penthouse, with its terrace overlooking the red-tiled rooftops of Venice, was designed as a vacation apartment for a young professional couple. In converting the former attic space, architect Federico Masotto opted for light materials that capture the colors of the Venetian landscape—faded whitewashed brickwork, terra-cotta plaster, and a palette that echoes dawn and dusk skies over the laguna. But he also wanted to embody the spirit of fantasy that is so much a part of the city's identity, and for this he designed a kitchen like no other. Described by Masotto as a "pop-shaped futuristic Venetian space-bubble," it was inspired by the fantastical drawings of Mœbius's *Venise Céleste*. Above a simple run of intense purple units, a triangular lime-green backsplash draws the eye up to an eccentric display of colored Plexiglas shapes based on drawings by visual artist Vava Dudu. As if that was not surreal enough, the mirrored section of the installation also conceals a large screen that can be unrolled for watching movies.

AMO
MOUR

The Venice-inspired colors inside the apartment find expression in the floor tiles of the terrace patio. Back inside, Vava Dudu's art can also be seen in the murals, screens, and curtains throughout the apartment

CONSTRUCTION VIA DECONSTRUCTION

Hoa's House · ioa studio · Melbourne, Australia

This open-plan kitchen/dining/living room has a wonderfully deconstructed quality to it, having once been an office space in a 150-year-old hotel. To maximize on space, the architects at ioa studio ripped out the ceiling lining and structure on the floor above to create a double-height space with an open mezzanine beneath a gable roof. Much of the exposed fabric of the original building has been left as found, and there are patches of old brick and cracked, hardened plaster beneath the Oregon rafters. Structural elements, such as exposed pipes and I-beams, are painted brightly to tie in with the Australian bush-inspired palette—greens and reds combined with rich timbers. The kitchen/dining room stands on a raised bed with a curved step down into the living room. Designed as a single unit, it combines cupboard storage with open shelves and has a cheerful terrazzo countertop and backsplash. Unique to the design is a pullout island bench that neatly slots into the whole when not in use. It is a playful design that echoes the deconstruction of the space around it.

FUN COLOR-BLOCKED BRUTALISM

York Way Penthouse · Studio Rhonda · London, United Kingdom

This open-plan kitchen was designed for the home of two professional chefs who also needed it to function as a space for demo classes and photo shoots. With a brief to create something "robust yet fun," Studio Rhonda settled on creating modular units based on the dimensions of the thick concrete tiles used for the kitchen tilework. At the heart of the design, a chunky kitchen island clad in steely gray and deep yellow tiles houses the cooking appliances. Beyond this, lining the walls of one corner of the room, is a run of built-in cabinets below a gray-tiled countertop and backsplash. Above is a set of open shelves, painted in brilliant white. At the far end of this run stand floor-to-ceiling cupboards, the doors painted bubblegum pink set within a pink-tiled frame. Central to the renovation of the entire apartment, the kitchen design sets the tone for the styling throughout. In the dining area of the room is a table with a green-tiled top, while the walls of the adjacent living room are painted with broad, gray and white stripes and feature a large geometric motif in the pink, yellow, and green shades of the tiles.

BUDGET RENOVATION WITH A NOVEL DECORATIVE SCHEME

Klinker Apartment · Serboli Bureau and Colombo Architecture · Barcelona, Spain

Rendered in a rich terra-cotta tone throughout, the kitchen in this Barcelona vacation home is like a hollow brick insert at the heart of the main living space—a tube, of sorts, that incorporates not just the kitchen/dining area, but also a small office space. All features of the kitchen, including the floor, backsplash, cabinets, and central island are finished in the same color. This unifies the space, but also defines those to either side—the living room and the entranceway. The design represents a novel solution to Serboli Bureau's and Colombo Arquitecture's brief, which was to renovate an apartment badly damaged by fire. The budget was tight, so there could be no major structural work. Much of the success of the entire renovation lies in what the architects call a "valance" that lines the walls, doors, and windows, "giving an artificial horizon, visually widening spaces in an otherwise vertically proportioned property." The soft palette takes its colors from the original tiled floors in the living room, the darkest hues of which have been applied to the living room and bedroom ceilings.

COOKING WITH SMART AND MINDFUL DESIGN

CHASSEUR

A successful kitchen needs to function properly and suit the specific needs of its user.
In some kitchens—particularly those in open-plan spaces—styling is as important as functionality.
Kitchens that are used less often need to be just as functional but can take up less space.

How much actual cooking takes place in a kitchen? The answer to this question determines not only the types of appliances included in a design, but also the amount of workspace given to food preparation.

A kitchen for one in an occasional vacation home requires different cooking facilities to that of a large family residence. Even then, some people cook all meals from scratch day after day, while others barely cook at all. Appliances might include a full range, an oven, a grill, a microwave, a stovetop, and/or all manner of additional gadgetsfrom steamers and air fryers to bread makers and toasters. Are they to be visible? And, if so, are branding and styling important? Or should they be integrated and as inconspicuous as possible? Their position in the kitchen is important too, ensuring that there is also adequate space for food preparation close by. The convention is to place an oven and stovetop fairly centrally, with the fridge to one side and the sink to the other. But there are many permutations, such as installing the oven and stovetop in a kitchen island, or having an oven set reasonably high up within a wall of cabinetry, or placing it between undercounter cabinets, below a stovetop and with a countertop on either side. On a practical level, wherever appliances are placed, ventilation and extraction need resolving, too.

Properly designed kitchens often have layouts that ensure they can run almost like a machine. For example, all the cooking activities can be centered on the kitchen island and all other needs—running water, utensils, ingredients—within easy reach. Charming elements, like the ladder below, make the cooking more enjoyable.

Whether the solution is a kitchen island, a little kitchenette, or a more conventional L-shape, beautiful design will always enhance the experience. There is always room for aesthetic pleasure in a kitchen.

A LIGHT TOUCH OF ART DECO STYLE

Bent Street · Kim Kneipp Studio · Kensington, Australia

Occupying one corner of a large open-plan space, the starting point for this kitchen design by Kim Kneipp Studio was an art deco-inspired bookcase that she designed for the same house several years earlier. Characterized by elegant custom joinery using recycled wood and a soft, natural palette of greens, browns, and grays, the kitchen is a harmonious collection of units of varied height. Extending surfaces here and there allow for extra shelving on the back wall and a breakfast bar on the island. The open-ended curved shelves, the rounded corners of the cabinetry, the mosaic-tiled backsplash, and the raw brass ladder rail are all reminiscent of the streamlined art deco style. Though the kitchen is compact, highly functional, and has plenty of storage, Kneipp has succeeded in making it feel light, airy, and aesthetically pleasing. Painting the upper cupboards white, for example, and tucking the sink behind a concealed cocktail bar in the island, makes them seem to disappear into the background.

With a keen eye for design, Kim Kneipp Studio has considered every last detail: the cabinets are adorned with custom wood handles, high storage is made accessible by a brass ladder rail, and the natural hues of the rush-seated barstools add an earthy touch.

SO GOOD, YOU COULD EAT IT!

The Fantales Kitchen · YSG Studio · Melbourne, Australia

The Fantales Kitchen was the result of an invitation by Australian manufacturer Laminex for YSG Studio to design a beautiful yet durable kitchen utilizing Laminex laminates. With the entire Laminex Color Collection at its disposal, YSG settled on a combination of solid-color laminates alongside classic woodgrains. Named after Fantales, a brand of chocolate-covered soft caramels beloved by many in Australia, the color scheme chosen by the studio is one of warm, velvety toffee browns. The primary task area consists of an L-shaped bench raised above a platform of glass mosaic tiles, set against a wall painted in a mottled, terra-cotta hue. The joinery is faced with laminate in "Burnt Ochre" and the countertop in "Moroccan Clay." A beautifully sculpted kitchen island is finished in three contrasting woodgrain laminates and features a striking decorative band of alternating strips of dark and light. As a whole, the kitchen demonstrates how flexible the laminates are in creating sculptural shapes, curved outlines, and interlocking patterns that define the design.

To contrast with the predominantly brown and orange of their kitchen design, YSG Studio lined the drawers and cabinet interiors with Laminex's Fresh Spring—a laminate in summer-sky blue.

HARMONY IN AN OPEN SPACE

East Village Apartment · GRT Architects · New York, NY, USA

In restructuring this apartment in an East Village building from the turn of the 20th century, GRT Architects have created distinct and discrete living, dining, and kitchen areas within an ostensibly open-plan space. The boundaries are subtle. Framed openings replace walls, and transitions are signaled simply by a change in flooring; the checkered tile of the kitchen gives way to parquet where the dining room starts, and a neat strip of herringbone demarcates the dining room/living room threshold. The design of the kitchen itself embraces its functionality with tiled surfaces, flush cabinetry, and a custom-made island to house electrical appliances. The finishes are soft and warm—brass fittings, white oak carpentry, and a satin white countertop. Cabinets are either raised above the floor or suspended from the ceiling on brass pins, allowing the kitchen to feel more fluid within the open-plan space and less "built-in." From here, although materials and colors shift from room to room, they do so in harmony and with recurring themes—brass elements and oversized door pulls—that tie the spaces together aesthetically.

A WES ANDERSON-INSPIRED SCOUTS CAMP CONCEPT

Camp Canoe · MR. Design Studio · Franschhoek, South Africa

When it was commissioned to design the interior for seven identical tents at the Canoe Camp glamping retreat in the Cape winelands of South Africa, MR. Design Studio relished the challenge of making the drab, khaki tent walls visually exciting. The whole venture is novel and quirky, with wood-fired hot tubs on the decking outside, a quilted wall above the bed and old luggage and backpacks serving as wall-mounted storage. The fun carries on in the kitchen, which is a neat modular design in one corner of the generous open-plan space. Modestly equipped, the kitchen features an integrated fridge, a sink, a small stovetop, and a short run of under-counter cupboards and drawers with over-sized knobs. A particular highlight is the "pegboard" backsplash into which are slotted pegs for suspending shelves or hanging mugs, kitchen utensils, and the like. Asked what they drew on for inspiration, MR. Design Studio answers without hesitation: "Swiss army knives, scout knots, survival essentials, and a touch of Wes."

THE MAKING OF A LIVED-IN MODERN AESTHETIC

11 Lynwood Project · Montana Labelle Design · Toronto, Canada

Central to Montana Labelle's interior design schemes are richly figured marbles, custom ceramics, and chunky pieces from her own product line, Montana Labelle Lifestyle. Often large-scale and with bold geometric and brutalist forms, it is easy to think that such pieces might feel too monumental to make for comfortable living spaces. But Labelle combines these things with vintage furniture and accessories and a soft, neutral palette that ranges from whites, creams, and grays, through dusky pinks and sage greens, to darker grays and browns. The effect is to conjure, in the designer's own words, "a more lived-in modern aesthetic." The 11 Lynwood Project is actually Labelle's own home, and it represents the very best of what she has to offer. In the kitchen, a Lacanche range lines one wall and low-level cabinets line another. Above them is a deep marble countertop as well as a backsplash and shelf made of high-relief ceramic tiles. On the entire length of the shelf stands a fine collection of vintage ceramics. The subtle and muted color palette stands out against the black, glazed-tile floor.

BRINGING DANISH STYLE TO LOWER MANHATTAN

Vipp Studio NYC · Vipp · New York, NY, USA

The Vipp Studio NYC is not just a showroom for the Danish firm's iconic V1 kitchen but is also the residence of third-generation Vipp owner Sofie Christensen Egelund, her husband Frank Christensen Egelund, and their family. Besides the kitchen, the apartment is also home to the couple's contemporary art collection and various other Vipp pieces, including several versions of the brand's Pedal Bin, originally designed in 1939 by Sofie's grandfather and Vipp founder, Holger Nielsen. The Egelunds moved to New York in 2014 in order to introduce the Vipp minimalist modular kitchen system to design-minded consumers in the United States. Housed in a former factory dating back to 1883, the studio has high ceilings and light streaming in from a wall of windows. The styling is minimalist, with whitewashed beams across the ceiling and exposed brickwork painted in shades of warm gray. It is the perfect backdrop for the sleek, black steel kitchen, which unfolds as a large island with two runs of identical drawers and an integrated stovetop against a backdrop of tall modules and Vipp's open rack system.

The sleek, minimalist styling of the kitchen finds echoes throughout the apartment—even in the art. Additional Vipp furnishings include a limestone Cabin Square Table, dining chairs, and Anglepoise lamps.

THE ART AND SCIENCE OF SERVING FOOD

For regular family mealtimes and entertaining, it can be nicer to eat in a separate dining room, away from the clutter of meal preparation. For things you make every day, such as coffee, or when preparing quick meals, it is always useful to have everything you need close at hand.

Once prepared, how will a meal be eaten? Depending on the time of day and the meal in question—breakfast, a snack, a lone lunch, supper with guests—various considerations influence how it is served.

For a kitchen to function at its best, all aspects of producing a meal—whether for dining alone, family sustenance, or entertaining—need thought, and this includes how best to serve food. In an open-plan kitchen, is there a dedicated space for enjoying a meal without diners directly overlooking the chaos created during its preparation? Or, if the kitchen is separate from the dining room, is there enough counter space for plating food up? A kitchen island can prove useful for the latter, providing a clear surface away from the main activity of preparing a meal. For less formal meals, or for dining alone, an island might also provide an uncluttered space at which to perch and eat. Another consideration is accessibility to glasses, crockery, cutlery, and other items for the table. For everyday meals, these things need to be close at hand, whereas for occasional, more formal events you can afford to store dinnerware in less accessible spots—difficult-to-reach cupboards or low-level shelving and drawers, for example.

Kitchen islands have multiple uses when it comes to serving. For example, if you are eating alone, perching at an island is less formal than sitting at a dining table. The island can also be used as a clutter-free plating-up station.

All sorts of fun can be had sourcing glassware, tableware, and accessories.
Whether it's the simple plates and glasses for everyday dining, fancy dinnerware for entertaining, or pulling out all the stops for a party, a well-dressed table makes the meal more enjoyable.

MEDITERRANEAN STYLING WITH A TRENDY TWIST

Cala Molí · Ibiza Interiors · Ibiza, Spain

This project involved not one but two kitchens for a midcentury house nestled between a creek and a pine forest in Ibiza. Taking its cues from the modern styling of the original home, the design by Ibiza Interiors blends the contemporary with more rustic features of the traditional Spanish finca. Inside, the raw materials of the stone-paved floors and richly grained wood of the kitchen cabinetry contrast with more refined surfaces such as the marble countertop and brass fixtures. Set on a drystone terrace and surrounded by wiry pine trees, oleanders, and agapanthus, the outdoor kitchen is built up against thick, whitewashed walls that are typical of the vernacular architecture. As with the indoor kitchen, the styling is a seamless blending of the traditional and the contemporary, with a brick oven and grill and a stone sink set within a strictly geometrical framework. Paired with a chunky wooden dining table beneath the trees, it completes this contemporary take on the rural Mediterranean lifestyle.

Throughout the design, rustic finishes combine with contemporary Scandinavian pieces for a serene, natural feel. A glass roof above the living area brightens the house during winter and makes it feel more connected to the garden in summer.

ENGLISH STYLING FOR RURAL LIVING

Kitchen in a Surrey Home · Maddalena Minerva · Surrey, United Kingdom

For the renovation of this large family home in Surrey, London-based design studio Maddalena Minerva took inspiration from both the surrounding countryside and traditional British design to create a kitchen that is as beautiful as it is practical. At one end of the kitchen stands a classic cast-iron range set within the white-tiled alcove of a faux chimney breast. The surrounding cabinetry is rendered in a rich dark green with antique brass fittings. At the other end of the kitchen is a walk-in pantry with striking emerald tiles and tongue-and-groove paneling. Between the two, beneath an impressive double-height pitched roof with exposed beams, a butler's sink is set within a sizable island complete with breakfast bar. The countertops are wood and Silestone—both durable and functional—the latter with gray-green veining to complement the green of the cabinets. In keeping with country kitchen tradition, Maddalena Minerva has used tumbled limestone pavers to line the kitchen floor, softening them with a Victorian-style runner for comfort.

The bespoke green of the cabinetry links to the colors in the garden and takes on different tones depending on the light. The art on the walls has been chosen to reflect the landscape of the countryside, making the room feel quintessentially English.

Kitchen in a Surrey Home

A CONTEMPORARY RETREAT BEHIND A HISTORIC FACADE

Crofters Cottage · Jan Henrik Jansen and Marshall Blecher · Nieby, Germany

From the street, this rafter's cottage looks much as it has since the late 1800s, with time-worn brick walls beneath a tidy thatched roof. Step inside, however, and a radical conversion at the hands of architects Jan Henrik Jansen and Marshall Blecher tells a different story. The cottage overlooks a nature reserve in northern Germany and was in an advanced state of disrepair when its current owners bought it. They wanted to preserve the historical appearance of the building but also wanted it to be a stylish, contemporary retreat for weekends. At the heart of the house were 14 small rooms with low ceilings that the architects opened up to create a large kitchen/dining area with a soaring ceiling. A long concrete island stands in the center of the room, morphing into a dining table at the far end. Juxtaposed with this ultra-modern intervention are historic elements that include the cottage's small mullioned windows and exposed oak rafters overhead. Joinery, doors, and furniture are custom made from German oak to match the floorboards.

BREATHING NEW LIFE INTO A HOME

Studio Cottage · Sun Min and Christian Taeubert · Beijing Outskirts, China

In this renovation of a rural cottage, fashion designer Sun Min and architect Christian Taeubert have introduced contemporary features and materials while maintaining the rustic simplicity of the original building. In the main living area—essentially a long, relatively narrow, open-plan unit flanking a courtyard—the couple has created a space that progresses seamlessly from living room to kitchen, dining room, and—raised on a small platform at the far end—a sleeping area. According to Min and Taeubert, "Developing rural areas is often less about preserving tradition and more about reviving, because the tradition is not really present." In keeping with this philosophy, Min and Taeubert have retained original features such as the exposed beams and mottled plaster walls, and have introduced modern elements that include a stainless-steel partition wall, sliding glass doors, and contemporary wire-frame lighting. The kitchen itself takes shape as a run of stainless-steel cabinets placed parallel to a simple wooden dining table flanked with Harry Bertoia's iconic midcentury wire chairs.

The contemporary elements sit comfortably in a room that is otherwise furnished with woven textiles and traditional utensils made of metal, earthenware, and wood. Colors are predominantly soft, muted, and natural.

A CONTEMPORARY KITCHEN DESIGN WITH RUSTIC UNDERTONES

Modern Farmhouse Kitchen · Husk · Bristol, United Kingdom

When asked to describe the starting point for the design of this kitchen, Millie Teden of Husk replies, "We designed this kitchen to work in a modern space but wanted to incorporate farmhouse features in keeping with the location of the property." The kitchen stands at one end of a space that also houses the dining room—a simple, rustically furnished area with tongue-and-groove paneling in a midnight blue. Husk's approach with the kitchen was to continue that simplicity, installing a long run of bespoke floor-to-ceiling smoked-oak cabinets paired with a large kitchen island with a laminate finish. While the cabinets match the color of the dining room, the island has a soft beige tone. Both are paired with beautifully figured Neolith countertops—the island in a style called Abu Dhabi and the back run in Ceppo. The sink and the state-of-the-art Fisher & Paykel kitchen appliances are neatly and discreetly inset so that lines are sleek and surfaces are flush. Soft, natural textiles and painted ceramics complete the look.

The Kingdom of quality

Husk's kitchen fronts work with Ikea's cabinet frames, which means their clients get a bespoke finish for a fraction of the price. For the sink alcove, Husk took inspiration from Italian Vogue Living.

A KITCHEN WITH A BRICK CENTERPIECE

Steam Brewery Conversion · Aux · Ghent, Belgium

In a large, open-plan space beneath a pitched roof, within a framework of hefty timber joists, exposed I-beams, and whitewashed brickwork, this industrial-style kitchen was designed as part of a conversion of a former brewery. The kitchen/dining area occupies a dedicated space within the home yet remains open to the living room on one side with views onto the roof garden on the other. Playing on the theme of the brickwork in which the original 19th-century building was built, the architects fashioned the kitchen as a brick sculpture that incorporates a plinth for the kitchen island and niches for cabinets and shelves, while concealing the more unsightly elements of a modern kitchen. The muted, earthy color of the stack-bonded brick walls matches that of the travertine flooring—a pale palette that contrasts with the black-stained wood of the cabinets in the niches and openings. The stainless-steel countertops and glass shelves add subtle industrial undertones, their cold surfaces offering a counterweight to the warmth of the flooring and brickwork.

The kitchen design references the brickwork of various bonds and sizes visible throughout the building. It is also a very sturdy and durable material, resistant to impact and strong enough for mounting shelves and cabinets.

A NEW KITCHEN IN THE SHAKER STYLE

The Chiswick Basement Kitchen · deVOL Kitchens and Clarence & Graves · London, United Kingdom

This spacious ground-floor kitchen combines deVol Kitchens' modular Shaker-style units with a sophisticated interior design by Clarence & Graves. As such, it presents a gracious blend of the traditional with the contemporary. Standing on a black-and-white checkered tile floor, a large island in the center of the room houses all the integrated appliances needed for cooking family meals. Below a beautifully veined marble countertop, the Shaker-style paneled doors have simple turned knobs and are painted a deep blue to match the run of cabinets on the far wall of the kitchen. Here, a large butler's sink is set within the chimney breast, the backsplash lined with marble to match the island. At the end of the run, open shelves rise to the ceiling and are backed with tongue-and-groove wood and lined with glassware, cookbooks, stockpots, and firewood. Additional storage space and an integrated fridge/freezer can be found in a wall of Shaker-style cabinetry in the adjoining alcove. Flooding the room with light, pistachio green Crittall windows and doors lead out to the garden.

The floor-to-ceiling Crittall doors and windows have the effect of doubling the size of the kitchen when the doors are open in summer. The pistachio green paintwork blends in with the foliage outside.

Placing the sink in the chimney breast enabled the designer to focus the cooking area around the island within easy reach of all of the kitchen's main facilities—the pantry, sink, and storage.

PALM SPRINGS MEETS ENGLISH SEASIDE ECCENTRICITY

Club Jupiter · Emma Jane Palin, Whinnie Williams, Anna Hart · Margate, United Kingdom

Created by interior stylist and writer Emma Jane Palin, journalist Anna Hart, and interior designer Whinnie Williams, Club Jupiter is a mobile-home renovation project that aims to bring new life to the U.K. travel and manufactured housing industry. At the heart of the design is the women's shared love of retro design, specifically the exuberance of Madonna Inn and the Palm Springs desert resort, both in California. Lined with green-and-white checkered Forbo flooring, the open-plan living, dining, and kitchen areas share an earthy palette of green, blue, orange, and brown, and feature a good number of upcycled and repurposed items. In the kitchen, new cabinet fronts were made for the existing units, the brass sink was found discarded, and a gold tap was salvaged from elsewhere in the original home, or caravan, as they are called in the United Kingdom. Animal print and bamboo wallpaper add a touch of Palm Springs glamour, proving, in the words of the creators, that "anyone can bring Hollywood vibes into even the smallest of spaces."

AN EXPRESSION OF HUMBLE LUXURY

Hutchinson Street · Kim Kneipp Studio · Brunswick East, Australia

This kitchen, designed by Kim Kneipp for her own family home, draws inspiration from the Japanese wabi-sabi design philosophy and, specifically, Jun'ichirō Tanizaki's essay on Japanese aesthetics, "In Praise of Shadows." A central theme here—and throughout the home—is the creation of intimate spaces in which soft lighting, small nooks, and areas of shadow conjure a sense of calm and quiet retreat. In the kitchen, white walls provide the backdrop for recycled wood cabinetry, a crystal-embedded countertop, and glossy black tiles. The result is a combination of shadowy, dark zones with pops of color and sparkle as the tiled and granite surfaces catch the light. The room leads out into a bamboo-lined internal courtyard, the bright green of the foliage serving to intensify the contrasts in the kitchen. In keeping with Kneipp's design philosophy, the look is humble and homey by design, and luxurious by finish. "Interiors are built to be perfectly imperfect, using materials that will age and patina over time, and textures intended to soften with wear," she says.

Clever details increase the functionality of the kitchen while maintaining the Japanese aesthetic. The crystal-filled granite countertop has an inset compost bin with a recycled wood lid, and behind the range hood lies a well-organized spice cabinet.

A HARMONIOUS MARRIAGE OF TWO STRUCTURES

Creek House · VFA Architecture + Design · Prince Edward County, Canada

This extension of a rural, 100-year-old barn in Ontario's Prince Edward County adopts the original vernacular with a red metal roof and an exterior of pre-stained wood siding, seamlessly integrating the new with the old. Inside, the walls and sloped ceilings of the tall, pitched roof are lined with bright white pine. Designed by VFA Architecture+Design, the structure provides a new living and entertaining space to support the practice of a celebrated professional chef. A major focus of the studio's brief was to source locally and repurpose as many materials as possible. Contrasting with the white pine, the structural beams, left raw and unfinished, are made from wood reclaimed from a local barn, while repurposed cherrywood makes up much of the kitchen shelving cabinetry, including the island. At the opposite end of this vast room, a chimney built with charcoal-colored concrete blocks extends the height of the extension, and black metal finishes introduce contemporary notes into the space.

The owner reclaimed the cherry wood from a tree on the farm. Full of irregularities and of different lengths and thicknesses, it was jig-sawed to produce shelves, cabinetry, and a custom island table in the kitchen.

AN INDUSTRIAL KITCHEN IN ANCIENT SURROUNDINGS

French Townhouse · Vipp · Uzès, France

In Chris and Lone McCourt's refurbished French medieval townhouse, a trio of Vipp kitchen modules—Island, Wall, and Tall—stand on the room's original dark stone floor. Made of steel and finished with a matte black powder coating, the units have an industrial appearance that sits well in this room, with its generous proportions and handsome wooden doors. The exposed beams across the ceilings have been whitewashed to match the walls, and contribute to the bright, clean, modern aesthetic of the space. The dining room is open to the kitchen and, while it is similar in proportion and interior decoration with beautiful stone floors and whitewashed walls, its furnishings are predominantly made of wood. An oak table is flanked by metal-framed plywood chairs on one side and a rustic wooden bench on the other, and a marble-topped, painted wood sideboard sits against the back wall. The industrial look carries through, however, in the 1920s teal enamel shades, originally from Chris's workshop in London, suspended above the dining table.

Chris McCourt is a furniture maker and among the many beautiful furnishings in this home are pieces from his own company, Isokon Plus, which specializes in reviving midcentury designs as well as producing pieces by new designers.

SITTING DOWN TO EAT WITH STYLE AND COMFORT

Bar stools are the obvious choice for placing at the edge of a kitchen island and they can be tucked away beneath the counter when not in use. Simple wooden chairs are suited to seating arrangements in rural settings—both inside and out.

Most kitchen designs include a dedicated space for eating meals. The shape this takes depends not only on the size of the room and the types of meals eaten there, but also on the room's overall styling.

Depending on the type of kitchen there are plenty of options for seating. At the very least, there may be space at one end of a countertop or a kitchen island that can serve as a breakfast bar, with a couple of high stools that tuck away neatly beneath the work surface when not in use. At the other end of the spectrum, there might be enough room to accommodate a dining table for four, six, or more people. For less formal areas, solutions might include built-in benches or booth seating, a small table with low stools, and, for kitchens that are very tight on space, foldaway furniture that can be stored against a wall or in a closet. There is much fun to be had in finding seating furniture that ties in with the overall styling of the kitchen. There is a wealth of iconic designs available in every conceivable material and color—from Thonet's bentwood chair to Starck's Louis Ghost to Jacobsen's Ant chair, the possibilities are limitless. Finding the right style is particularly important if the kitchen is part of a wider, open-plan space that also features the living room.

For large kitchens and those that open into a dining area, long tables with sets of matching or mismatched chairs offer the best of both worlds for growing families and stylish party entertaining.

Small spaces require innovative solutions. Round tables take up less space and work well with built-in bench seating. Studio Merlin's renovation (top right) of a London apartment includes an informal recessed sitting space at one end of the kitchen counter.

WEEKLY OFFERINGS
Nigel Slater Real Food
JAMIE'S GREAT BRITAIN
ITALY
Veg
JAMIE'S 15-MINUTE MEALS
OTTOLENGHI SIMPLE
rick stein's seafood
Nigel Slater
PLENTY
JAMIE OLIVER
NIGELLA CHRISTMAS

A KITCHEN FULL OF WARMTH AND COLOR

Cozy Family Kitchen · Pluck · Harborne, United Kingdom

This kitchen is a large, open space, flooded with natural light from all directions, which flows naturally into the dining room and living room. In giving the space a much-needed makeover, the homeowners sought the expertise of Pluck studio, whose signature look combines bespoke cabinetry in an impressive range of colored and wood-veneered finishes with open shelving and glass-front cabinets. Here, the modular units with flush fronts and recessed handles are finished in veneers in Market Mustard, Ruskin Blossom, and Cherry Wood. The colors work well to bring warmth to the space, the softness of the Ruskin Blossom acting as a perfect counter to the intensity of the Market Mustard. At the heart of the room stands an island at which family members can perch and chat while cooking. The owners needed ample storage, so Pluck introduced clever interventions to prevent the space feeling too "built-in," such as their custom-made Spoke shelves, a fluted glass cabinet, and a bookshelf at the front of the island, itself offering a neat transition to the living/dining area.

The clients opted to leave the ceiling joists exposed and painted the whole area white. This had a dramatic effect on the room, adding character and height and transforming an otherwise nondescript element of the space into a desirable feature.

BLURRING THE BOUNDARIES BETWEEN INSIDE AND OUT

Grote Hond · Poot Architectuur · Antwerp, Belgium

In this timeless extension of a spacious mansion house in Antwerp's belle epoque neighborhood of Zurenborg, the undisputed star of the show is the marble tiling, reclaimed from North Station in Brussels. This elegant, noble material suits the classic styling of this period house perfectly, but as it is paired with steel, glass, concrete, and wood, it is contemporary at the same time. Inspired by the work of Mies van der Rohe and Juliaan Lampens, the almost double-height extension is constructed primarily from steel and glass, the design allowing Poot Architectuur to carry the marble through into the rear garden, seamlessly blurring the lines between inside and outside. The architects have used the marble to create a massive sculpture within the rear facade, uniting built-in benches outside with the countertop and kitchen furniture inside. Inside, the kitchen color palette is subtle and sophisticated, combining a range of whites and grays with the mellower tones of the wooden floor in the dining room.

The marble elements inside and outside the house match the height of the kitchen countertop, further reinforcing the relationship between the house and the garden. The architects have also taken care to make sure the proportions are in harmony with those of the existing building.

MINIMAL INDUSTRIAL MEETS TECHNO TROPICAL

FlagFlat · Garrastudio and dos42 · Murcia, Spain

Inspired by the homemade political flags that often hang on Spanish balconies, dos42 and Garrastudio's FlagFlat is a 3D rendering of a "flag" that represents their different aesthetics and approaches to the design process. Dissected in places by sliding doors, the large, open space is divided into four strips along its length, starting at the entrance to the apartment, so that Garrastudio's Memphis and "techno tropical" stripes alternate with dos42's minimal industrial and Nordic stripes. Each is defined by its choice of materials and colors. At one end, the kitchen straddles the two zones and connects directly to the living room and an outdoor terrace. Dominant features are the tutti-frutti oranges and greens and the striking Venetian terrazzo used for the countertop and floor. Since the stripes span the whole apartment, these materials and colors are repeated through the living room and find echoes in the bathroom on the other side of the living room wall. "It reminds us of the apartments from the 1960s in the area, with a design twist," say the architects.

The four sections of the apartment are clearly defined by their floor and ceiling decoration. While Garrastudio's Techno Tropical section is largely '60s inspired, the Memphis strip has a distinctly postmodern aesthetic, as is suggested by its name.

WARMTH, COLOR, AND CONTINUITY

CC Residence · Dries De Malsche · Cascais, Portugal

Bold geometry and strong earthy colors are the hallmarks of this kitchen in a Portuguese family holiday home. The work of Belgian interior designer Dries De Malsche, the design is part of a wider commission to renovate the entire interior of what De Malsche describes as a "rather soulless new-build villa." The styling in the kitchen is clean and minimal. Set against a dark mineral plaster floor, buff-colored walls and cabinets combine with floor-to-ceiling cupboards finished in brushed oak and an island fashioned from striking red travertine. The kitchen shares the ground floor of the home with a dining room, living room, master bedroom, and a spare room. All of the elements that take shape in the kitchen find expression elsewhere in the apartment. Wide openings between the main spaces (with sliding doors for privacy) allow sightlines from one end of the apartment to the other, emphasizing the continuity of styling and materials as you move from one room to the next.

Furnishings are minimal throughout the apartment and have a style reminiscent of Japanese design. Low-level tables made from dark wood and seating furniture upholstered in neutral textiles all have simple, geometric shapes.

CABINET-MAKING WITH NEW STYLING

Framed · Garde Hvalsøe · Copenhagen, Denmark

Based in Copenhagen, Garde Hvalsøe curates highly sophisticated bespoke interiors featuring exquisite hand-crafted furniture of their own design. Framed, a kitchen island housing built-in drawers and an integral sink, epitomizes their style. Drawing on a long tradition of Danish furniture design, this unit presents a harmonious combination of ancient natural materials, traditional cabinet-making, and contemporary styling. A set of solid ash drawers is suspended within a beautifully patinated copper frame that also serves as a countertop. Joined with hidden dovetail joints, and with slightly recessed partitions, the drawers appear to float within the frame. Gaps between them act as grips, allowing the grain of the wood on the drawer fronts to run uninterrupted across the front of the cabinet. The copper is reminiscent of traditional kitchenware and, combined with the wood, reflects Garde Hvalsøe's ethos to use "natural materials that provide inspiration due to their textural quality, diversity, and historical roots."

MINIMALIST STYLING FOR A FAMILY KITCHEN

Wiedeweltsgade · Nicolaj Bo · Copenhagen, Denmark

Bespoke furniture makers Nicolaj Bo made clever use of a relatively small floorplan to craft a minimalist kitchen/dining area on the ground floor of this 19th-century townhouse in the picturesque Copenhagen neighborhood of Kartoffelrækkerne. Sliding glass doors, based on the firm's Classic range, open onto a rear patio, and the room is made up of a kitchen island with an integrated sink and stovetop and a wall of cabinetry that wraps around the house's inner structural walls. With the exception of an espresso machine and a run of shelves housed in a niche, all appliances and storage spaces are concealed in the units, keeping lines minimal and lean while utilizing the available space to the max. A sophisticated palette combines a mushroom linoleum finish for the cabinetry with a "Jura" gray stone countertop and solid wood and veneer for the shelving and cabinet interiors. In the dining room stands an oak plank table with a bench seat that serves as extra storage space. All cabinetry and furnishings were custom-made locally by Nicolaj Bo.

The innovative design for the cabinetry lines the dining area as well as the kitchen and incorporates a concealed cabinet containing cutlery and glasses. A built-in radiator concealed within the same unit ensures that the lines remain sleek and uninterrupted.

CLASSIC DANISH DESIGN—SOFT, MATTE, AND TIMELESS

Hareskovby · Nicolaj Bo · Copenhagen, Denmark

In this newly built Danish villa, a sizable kitchen/dining area occupies the whole of the lower ground floor. Spacious and bright, its rear wall is sandwiched between two sets of steps leading up to the living room, establishing a comfortable, circular flow between the two rooms. Custom-made by Nicolaj Bo furniture makers, the kitchen itself comprises two timber-framed volumes finished in a soft, matte, steel-blue linoleum; a rear wall volume that combines low-level cupboards and drawers with a ceiling-height unit at one end; and a central volume that serves as a kitchen island with a sink, plenty of workspace, and a seating area. Both of these volumes stand on gray cement tiles that lead into a dining area framed by windows overlooking the garden. A set of light oak shelves on the rear wall contributes to the spacious feeling of the room and prevents the cabinetry from becoming too dominant. Overhead, the ceiling is lined with oak slats, a feature that softens the room both aesthetically and acoustically.

In designing a kitchen that fits precisely between the two sets of steps that lead to the house's living area, Nicolaj Bo managed to give the impression that the house was built around their creation and not vice versa.

A DESIGN THAT POINTS TO THE SKY

WKA Penthouse · Bruno Spaas Architectuur · Antwerp, Belgium

Designed by Bruno Spaas, this kitchen is at the heart of a penthouse apartment that is wrapped in glass and lined with mirrors. Fifteen floors up, every inch of the 3,700 ft^2 (350 m^2) apartment's flooring is made from chunks of locally sourced stone. The rest of the interior design is no less unconventional: a distortion-free tempered mirror and high-gloss painted surfaces create a sense of infinite space with their reflections. Besides a few load-bearing walls and doors to divide the areas and add privacy when needed, the entire space is a continuous loop and incorporates clever storage solutions to keep furnishings at a minimum. Reduced to little more than a pair of islands, the kitchen exemplifies the styling throughout. Here, as in the foyer bench and the bathtub in the master bathroom, the customized pieces are constructed from vertically arranged strips of locally produced Belgian terrazzo. Underlining the verticality of the tower, the same visual expression is repeated in the painted woodwork, lending a common language to the design.

Cushions, decorative items, and drawer and cupboard linings in pops of intense green and blue are interspersed among the predominantly brown and stone shades that set the tone for the apartment.

A STRIKING TRANSITION FROM OLD TO NEW

Townhouse Conversion and Extension · Justies Architekten BDA · Freiburg im Breisgau, Germany

A state-of-the-art extension, with a nod to brutalism in its design, reestablishes a long-lost physical connection between the first floor of this turn-of-the-century townhouse and the basement-level garden at the rear. The design gives the clients increased living space inside and out, and places the kitchen at the heart of the home—an important factor, given their passion for cooking. The apartment is one of four in a listed building, which meant Justies Architekten had to retain its original structure and external appearance, but had considerable flexibility in the design of the extension. Cast in-situ, it consists of two overlapping, identically sized concrete rectangles. The first houses the kitchen/dining area and the second serves as the garden terrace. The transition from inside to out is an important one. The terrace, steps, and bench continue the minimalist materiality of the kitchen area, while floor-to-ceiling sliding windows blur the boundaries between inside and out.

The basement garden and sunken patio can be reached directly from the kitchen and from a terrace on the level above. A round skylight on the upper terrace of the cube provides additional daylight in the space below.

MATERIAL COMPLEXITY IN GEOMETRIC SPACES

Residence 0110 · Raúl Sánchez Architects · Barcelona, Spain

There is neat geometry at play in architect Raúl Sánchez's renovation of his own Barcelona apartment, Residence 0110. In this transformation of an existing apartment in a chamfered block, Sánchez has placed a square space housing the kitchen, living room, and dining room at the heart of his design. An adjacent triangular space accommodates the turn of the chamfer, beyond which lie two bedrooms and a bathroom. In creating these spaces Sánchez replaced most of the existing structural elements—all that remains is one corner of an old wall. It was retained out of necessity, but its position, in the middle of the main living space, also marks the boundaries between the kitchen/dining area and the rest of the space. Within his geometric spaces, Sánchez has made much use of color and materials to help define different areas, but also to tie them together: the black-stained oak of the kitchen cabinets also lines several walls of the living room; a bookcase on one wall is set within a pale pink frame; the central pillar is wrapped in highly polished brass; and all of the doors—whether leading to the rooms beyond or fronting the kitchen cabinets—are made of stainless steel.

Sánchez has furnished his apartment with custom-made items such as the leather sofa, brass pieces, and a marble washbasin, interspersed with design favorites that include a Vitra LCW armchair and the iconic Butterfly chair.

PURE HANDCRAFTED ELEGANCE

Layer · Garde Hvalsøe and Baks Arkitekter · Aarhus, Denmark

Designed by Baks Arkitekter, and called the In Situ House, this Danish villa is made of just three components: concrete, wood, and glass. Raw concrete walls inside and out frame floor-to-ceiling windows lined with warm oak. Inside, rooms of harmonious proportions are light and bright, with tall internal doors, also made of oak, and minimal furnishings. For the kitchen, the architects worked in collaboration with Garde Hvalsøe to create the Layer model. Key to the design, as elsewhere in the villa, are the Dinesen Layers oak panels used to make the central island and ceiling-height cabinets lining the wall. The elegant craftsmanship hearkens back to midcentury Danish design. All superfluous details have been pared away—there are no plinths, grips, or visible joints—allowing the natural beauty of the wood to stand out. The wood is a rich honey color that brings a warmth to the overall design, and it has been worked so that the grain runs vertically toward the ceiling to reflect, in the words of Garde Hvalsøe, "the surrounding forest's skyward direction."

Baks Arkitekter have maintained great unity in proportion and scale throughout. While the house itself is essentially linear in design, the floor-to-ceiling windows and doors give the rooms a real sense of verticality.

The styling in the kitchen finds echoes in other rooms of the house. Although the spaces are minimally furnished, there is plenty of warmth in the natural materials used—stone, wood, textiles—and in the soft light and neutral palette.

THE ELEGANCE OF OAK AND DOLOMIA STONE

Kitchen at Villa Altrove · Gregorio Pecorelli · Pognana Lario, Italy

This elegant 19th-century villa reflects, both inside and out, the subtle tones of the landscape that surrounds it on the banks of Lake Como in northern Italy's Lombardy region. The kitchen occupies a small corner of the ground floor and looks out across a beautiful garden with a swimming pool and a terrace overlooking the lake. With full-height, custom-designed cabinets finished in natural oak, and high-end integrated appliances, this is a discreet and contemplative space, fulfilling the client's brief for a room that is humble yet refined. The villa originally had lots of wooden elements, and designer Gregorio Pecorelli uses wood as an echo of the past. For the countertop, backsplash, and the large sink beneath the kitchen window, Pecorelli has also introduced Dolomia stone, which is often found in the churches and houses in the region. The colors are soft and the light is gentle and diffuse, giving the space, in Pecorelli's words, "the magical reverberation of the lake."

Tiled floors, walls without baseboards, and a neutral palette epitomize a style that the architect describes as "discretion and sobriety." Yet, throughout, the minimalism is softened by the warm, natural tones of the oak.

A

AGIUS SCORPO ARCHITECTS
@agiusscorpo

Studio 1
Fitzroy, Australia
Photography by Tom Ross
@tomross.xyz
pp. 30 bottom right, 76 bottom

AUX
@aux.be

Steam Brewery Conversion
Ghent, Belgium
Photography by Luc Roymans
roymans.com
pp. 174 – 177

AYROMLOO DESIGN
@jessica_ayromloo

Mexico City Residence
Mexico City, Mexico
Photography by Annie Schlechter / Interior Archive
@annieschlechter
pp. 96 top, 110 – 111

B

BLAF ARCHITECTEN
@blafarchitecten

House hkZ
Zoersel, Belgium
Photography by Stijn Bollaert
@stijn_bollaert
pp. 95, 98 – 101, 128 bottom

BRUNO SPAAS ARCHITECTUUR
@brunospaas

WKA Penthouse
Antwerp, Belgium
Photography by Jeroen Verrecht
@jeroenverrecht
pp. 131 top left, 230 – 233

D

DEVOL KITCHENS and CLARENCE & GRAVES
@devolkitchens
@clarenceandgraves

The Chiswick Basement Kitchen
London, United Kingdom
Photography by deVOL Kitchens
pp. 127, 130 top, 178 – 183

DGN STUDIO
@d_g_n_s

Magpie House
London, United Kingdom
Photography by Tim Crocker
@timcrockerphotographer
pp. 29, 52 – 55, 93

DRIES DE MALSCHE
@dries_de_malsche

CC Residence
Cascais, Portugal
Photography by Piet-Albert Goethals
@piet.albert.goethals
pp. 6 right, 216 – 219

DRIES OTTEN
@driesotten

Lardo Lyma
Antwerp, Belgium
Photography by Dries Otten
pp. 24 – 25

E

EMMA JANE PALIN, WHINNIE WILLIAMS, ANNA HART
@clubjupiteruk

Club Jupiter
Margate, United Kingdom
Photography by Joanna Bongard
@joannabongardphoto
pp. 155 top right, 184 – 185

F

FEDERICO MASOTTO ARCHITECTE
@federicomasotto_architecte

Venetian Penthouse
Venice, Italy
Photography by Philippe Garcia
@philippegarciaphotography
pp. 116 – 119

G

GARDE HVALSØE
@gardehvalsoe

Framed
Copenhagen, Denmark
Photography by Heidi Lerkenfeldt
@heidi.lerkenfeldt
pp. 31 top left, 76 top right, 220 – 221

GARDE HVALSØE and BAKS ARKITEKTER
@gardehvalsoe

Layer
Aarhus, Denmark
Photography by Birgitta Bjørnvad Wolfgang
@birgittawolfgang
pp. 30 bottom left, 242 – 247

GARRASTUDIO and DOS42
@garra.studio
@dos42arq

FlagFlat
Murcia, Spain
Photography by David Frutos
@davidfrutosphoto
pp. 74 bottom, 202 bottom left, 212 – 215

GREGORIO PECORELLI
@gregoriopecorelli

Kitchen at Villa Altrove
Pognana Lario, Italy
Photography by Francesca Iovene
@francescaiovene
pp. 152 top left, 248 – 251

GRT ARCHITECTS
@grtarchitects

East Village Apartment
New York, NY, USA
Photography by Nicole Franzen
@nicole_franzen
pp. 7 left, 140 – 141, 154 top

IOA STUDIO
@ioa_studio

Hoa's House
Melbourne, Australia
Photography by Tom Ross
@tomross.xyz
pp. 120 – 121

Hutchinson Street
Brunswick East, Australia
Photography by Lisa Cohen
@lisacohenphoto
pp. 130 bottom right, 186 top, 187 – 189
Photography by Eve Wilson
@evegwilson
pp. 186 bottom

H

HEIM BALP ARCHITEKTEN
@heimbalp

Gutshof Güldenhof
Stechlin, Germany
Photography by Francesca Iovene
@francescaiovene
pp. 56 – 59

HOLLOWAY LI
@_hollowayli

Highbury Apartment
London, United Kingdom
Photography by Edmund Dabney
@edmund_dabney
pp. 6 left, 10 – 13

HUSK
@madebyhusk

Modern Farmhouse Kitchen
Bristol, United Kingdom
Photography by
Brett Charles Photography
@brettcharlesphoto
pp. 8 left, 128 top left, 154 bottom left, 155 bottom, 170 – 173, 199

I

IBIZA INTERIORS
@ibizainteriors

Cala Molí
Ibiza, Spain
Photography by Ariadna Puigdomenech
@aripuigdomenech
pp. 156 – 159, 201

J

JAN HENRIK JANSEN
and MARSHALL BLECHER
@marshallblecher

Crofters Cottage
Nieby, Germany
Photography by José Campos
@josecamposphotographer
pp. 164 – 165

JUSTIES ARCHITEKTEN BDA
@justiesarchitekten

Townhouse Conversion and Extension
Freiburg im Breisgau, Germany
Photography by Annika Feuss
@feussfotografie
pp. 202 top, 234 – 237

K

KILO/HONČ
@kilo_honc

Loft
Bratislava, Slovakia
Photography by Matej Hakár
@matejhakar
pp. 31 bottom, 73, 86 – 89

KIM KNEIPP STUDIO
@kim.kneipp

Bent Street
Kensington, Australia
Photography by Lisa Cohen
@lisacohenphoto
pp. 130 bottom left, 132 – 135

M

MADDALENA MINERVA
@maddalenaminerva

Kitchen in a Surrey Home
Surrey, United Kingdom
Photography by Astrid Templier
@astridtemplier
pp. 31 top right, 160 – 163, 200 top right

MJÖLK ARCHITEKTI
@mjolk_architekti

Glass Cabin
Polubný, Czech Republic
Photography by BoysPlayNice
@boysplaynice
pp. 106 – 109

MOLLY MAHON
@mollymahonblockprinting

Deerhyrst Kitchen
Forest Row, United Kingdom
Photography by Emma Lewis
@emmalewisphotographer
pp. 68 – 71

MONTANA LABELLE DESIGN
@montanalabelle

11 Lynwood Project
Toronto, Canada
Photography by Patrick Biller
@patrickbiller
pp. 144 – 145

MR. DESIGN STUDIO
@instabymr

Camp Canoe
Franschhoek, South Africa
Photography by Inge Prins @inge_prins
pp. 77 bottom left, 142 – 143

STUDIO BEN ALLEN
@studitopallen

The House Recast
London, United Kingdom
Photography by
FRENCH+TYE
@frenchandtye
pp. 112 – 115

STUDIO HOKA
@hoka_projects

Studio H
Warsaw, Poland
Photography by
Magda Motrenko
und Maciej Sawczak
pp. 32 – 33, 75
Photography by
Dymitr Kalasznikow
@dimetriush
p. 28 bottom

STUDIO MERLIN
@studiomerlin

Maison pour Dodo
London, United Kingdom
Photography by Richard Chivers
@richchiversphoto
pp. 14 – 17,
94 top left und right,
203 top right

STUDIO RHONDA
@studio_rhonda

York Way Penthouse
London, United Kingdom
Photography by
Rachael Smith Photography ltd
@rachaelsmithphotographyltd
pp. 122 – 123,
155 top left

SUN MIN and CHRISTIAN TAEUBERT
@guobaner_beijing

Studio Cottage
Beijing Outskirts, China
Photography by Boris Shiu
borisshiuphoto.com
pp. 9 right,
131 top right,
154 bottom right,
166 – 169

T

TENHACHI ARCHITECT & INTERIOR DESIGN

Tenhachi House
Tokyo, Japan
Photography by Akihide Mishima
@akihidemishima
pp. 74 top right, 77 top

U

UNCOMMON PROJECTS
@uncommon_projects

Bespoke Kitchen and Study
London, United Kingdom
Photography by Jocelyn Low
@aformermagpie
pp. 27, 44 – 47

V

VFA ARCHITECTURE + DESIGN
@vfarchitect

Creek House
Prince Edward County,
Canada
Photography by Cindy Blazevic
pp. 30 top,
96 bottom right,
190 – 193

VIPP
@vipp

French Townhouse
Uzès, France
Photography by Anders Hviid
@andershviid
pp. 194 – 197

Vipp Studio NYC
New York, NY, USA
Photography by Adrian Gaut
@a_gaut
und Pernille Loof
@pernilleloof
pp. 146 – 149

Y

YSG STUDIO
@ysg.studio

The Fantales Kitchen
Melbourne, Australia
Photography by Derek Swalwell
@derek_swalwell
pp. 8 right, 28 top right,
97 top right, 131 bottom,
136 – 139, 152 top right

Budge Over Dover
Sydney, Australia
Photography by Prue Ruscoe
@prueruscoe
p. 202 bottom right

Z

ZLY ARCHITEKT
@zlyarchitekt

Apartment R405
Bratislava, Slovakia
Photography by Zly architekt
pp. 36 – 39, 77 bottom right

p. 152 bottom
Kseniya Ovchinnikova /
Getty Images

KITCHEN INTERIORS

New Spaces and Designs for Cooking and Dining

This book was conceived, edited, and designed by gestalten.

Edited by Robert Klanten and Masha Erman
Editorial support by Effie Efthymiadi

Preface by Jeppe Christensen, Reform
Text by Anna Southgate

Editorial Management by Anna Diekmann

Design, Layout, and Cover by Stefan Morgner

Photo Editor: Zoe Paterniani

Typefaces: Apoc by Matthieu Salvaggio, Basic Sans by Daniel Hernández, Times New Roman by Stanley Morison und Victor Lardent

Cover image by Tim Hirschmann/OTTO

Printed by appl druck GmbH, Wemding
Made in Germany

Published by gestalten, Berlin 2023
ISBN 978-3-96704-120-0

Bibliographic information published by the Deutsche Nationalbibliothek. The Deutsche Nationalbibliothek lists this publication in the Deutsche Nationalbibliografie; detailed bibliographic data is available online at www.dnb.de

None of the content in this book was published in exchange for payment by commercial parties or designers; gestalten selected all included work based solely on its artistic merit.

This book was printed on paper certified according to the standards of the FSC®.

MIX
Paper | Supporting responsible forestry
FSC® C004592